Running ever faster down the wrong road

Frank Coffield

First published in 2007 by the Institute of Education, University of London,
20 Bedford Way, London WC1H 0AL
www.ioe.ac.uk/publications

© Institute of Education, University of London 2007

Photograph of Professor Frank Coffield © North News Pictures 1999

British Library Cataloguing in Publication Data:
A catalogue record for this publication is available from the British Library

ISBN 978 0 85473 772 7

Design and typeset by info@chapmandesign.net
Printed by DSI Colourworks

Institute of Education • University of London

Running ever faster
down the wrong road
An alternative future for Education and Skills

Frank Coffield
Professor of Education

Based on an inaugural professorial lecture delivered at the Institute of Education,
University of London on 5 December 2006

Professor Frank Coffield

Introduction

I would like to begin with a confession. When it comes to inaugurals, I am a serial offender, a recidivist, having delivered one at Durham (Coffield, 1982) and Newcastle Universities (Coffield, 1999). So I also wish to begin with a promise to myself, to my family and to this audience: this is my third and last. Three strikes and out. I have found the cure; it is called retirement. I would like to consider this as both an inaugural and a valedictory lecture. '*Ave atque vale*'. Hello and goodbye. That was the first sentence I learned in Latin more than 50 years ago in Glasgow. I have not needed to use the phrase until tonight, which just goes to show how useful a general education is. You never know the day or the hour.

I would also like to begin with another promise and a health warning. I promise that the next hour will pass without another mention of 'transformational visions', 'stakeholders', 'step changes' or 'strategic purchasing functions', except when I quote disapprovingly from official sources or research reports. The phrase, 'strategic purchasing function' simply means a shopping list, but government departments need to imagine they are involved in a much grander enterprise. We tend to ridicule these phrases when we first hear them, but within a few months we are using them. In this way, these pretentious inanities vitiate our language, our thinking and our culture. The case I present tonight will be made in clear, simple English, which is one of our most potent weapons in the battle of ideas, but one which is, I think, decreasingly used by researchers.

Every discipline has its own technical vocabulary, but I suspect that we academics fail to communicate with a wider public by using such terms as 'co-configuration', when we mean involving practitioners as equal partners in the formation of new policy or practice. Such terms seem to be introduced to give a specious profundity to ideas which are in themselves relatively simple to understand. As Basil Bernstein once said to me: 'Coffield, you'll never get

1

anywhere in this game if you insist on writing in clear, simple English. Invent a few neologisms and the world will begin to treat you seriously.'

Let me present a brief overview of my argument and, in doing so, I am finally going to break with the self-denying ordinance of a lifetime and say what I really think. My case is that the government's programme of reform in the public services, despite significant investments and successes, is now doing more harm than good. It needs to be fundamentally redesigned and later I will briefly outline a few proposals for a different system. But first, we must stop running faster and faster down the wrong road. The destination is inappropriate, the curriculum out-dated, the policing too heavy and the determination to put the foot down even harder on the accelerator is a symptom of a dangerous machismo, best left to *Top Gear* presenters.

In one lecture it is not possible to deal with all the reforms which have been introduced into the public services since the 1980s. I cannot even deal with the reforms of the education service as a whole, but instead will confine myself to the post-compulsory sector, hereafter known as the Learning and Skills Sector (LSS), with the exception of higher education (HE). All the examples I quote shall be from that sector. The same fault lines or, to change the metaphor, the same malaises, run through the reform agenda of government whether they affect the primary, secondary, higher education or post-compulsory sector (or the health service or the probation service, for that matter). It may be consoling to those working in the other educational 'silos' to hear that their problems are replicated in another sector. But I want to offer more than consolation; I want to offer hope.

Now the health warning for those of you who have never been inside the LSS before. It is a vast and complex world which is restructured so frequently that it has become a full-time job just to read about the latest turns and twists of policy, never mind respond to them. So when I invite you to step into the LSS, remember to hold on to your mind in case you lose it. As your guide, I promise not to leave you on the other side but will lead you back safely, after a brief excursion into this fascinating, turbulent, insecure but desperately important world; a world which remains invisible to most politicians, academics and commentators because, with very few exceptions, neither they nor their children have ever passed through it.

Background

England does not have an educational system, but instead three badly co-ordinated sectors – schools, post-compulsory education and HE – which reflect sharp divisions within the Department for Education and Skills (DfES). The mental image suggested by these structural arrangements is of three well-intentioned but dyspraxic and myopic elephants, who are constantly bumping into each other and standing on each other's feet instead of interweaving smoothly in one elegant dance.

The post-compulsory sector has been aptly termed 'the neglected middle child between universities and schools' by Sir Andrew Foster (2005: 58). That neglect has, however, begun to be addressed since 1997 by the keen interest taken by the New Labour government. My first task is to show how the weaknesses in the present arrangements now outweigh the strengths; the second, more demanding, job is to suggest ways in which this internally fragmented *sector* could be slowly turned into a well-integrated *system* with a capacity to learn.

The data for both sections of this paper – the critique and the alternative – are, whenever possible, drawn from the research project, entitled *The Impact of Policy on Learning and Inclusion in the New Learning and Skills Sector*, which is part of the Teaching and Learning Research Programme, funded by the Economic and Social Research Council (ESRC).[1] Right at the outset I want to acknowledge that what follows draws on the work of a team of eight staff, but only the present author should (or will want to) be held responsible for the views expressed here.[2] Our project has now carried out more than 83 interviews of senior policy makers and officials of the key organisations at national, regional and local levels, as well as 4/5 rounds of visits to 24 learning sites (12 in the North East and 12 in London) in further education colleges, adult and community learning centres and work-based learning (see Figure 1). We have interviewed more than 300 learners and more than 200 managers, tutors and union learning reps. We have also analysed so far more than 350 central policy texts, as well as ministerial speeches, letters and press articles which cover the period from 1997 to 2006, all seeking to explain and legitimate government policy. In addition, our thinking has been influenced by numerous books, articles and reports by researchers and commentators who specialise in post-16 education.

From the very beginning we set ourselves the task of outlining the main characteristics of effective, equitable and inclusive local learning *systems*; and at the end I shall offer a preliminary response which I hope will be improved through public debate and dialogue. It is no part of my case, however, that there are no major building blocks already in place and I shall begin by briefly reviewing existing strengths.

Charting the impact of government policy on practice has not been, however, a simple matter of recording linear, evolutionary, coherent or cumulative progress. Rather, the processes of change have been complex, uneven, dynamic, ambiguous, hotly contested and often contradictory. Policies have not only evolved or been radically altered as Secretaries of State and senior civil servants have come and gone, but some policies were abandoned, while others were from the start internally inconsistent or flatly contradicted existing policies.

The writings of John Clarke and Janet Newman (Clarke and Newman, 1997; Newman, 2000, 2001, 2005) make clear that no one dominant model is being imposed from above – the picture is far more complicated than that. For example, Newman has produced a framework which represents four different models of governance, and government policy draws on all four.[3] Change, therefore, as enacted by New Labour, is a multidimensional, dynamic and conflictual process; top-down control and an obsession with targets have also intensified since my second inaugural in 1999, taking England much further in the wrong direction than either Scotland or Wales.

Figure 1 Levels within the Learning and Skills Sector

1	**International Level** e.g. European Commission, OECD
2	**National Level – Central Government** e.g. No. 10 and HM Treasury
3	**National Level – Departments** e.g. DfES, DTI, DWP
4	**National Level – 'arms-length' agencies (NDPBs)** e.g. National LSC, QIA, QCA, ALI, Ofsted, SSC and Independent Organisations e.g. Awarding Bodies, Unions, CBI
5	**Regional Level** e.g. Regional LSCs, RDAs
6	**Local Level** e.g. LSC Partnership Teams, 14–19 Network

	FE		**ACL**		**WBL**
7	**Institutional Level** e.g. College Principals	7	**Centre** e.g. Manager	7	**Firm** e.g. MD
8	**Departmental Level** e.g. Faculties, SfL Teams	8	**Course Level** Leader	8	**Training Dept** e.g. Training Manager, ULR
9	**Course Level** e.g. Managers, Leaders	9	**Classroom Level** Tutors	9	**Classroom Level** Tutors
10	**Classroom Level** e.g. Teachers	10	**Learners**	10	**Learners**
11	**Learners**				

KEY
FE Further education
ACL Adult and Community Learning
WBL Work Based Learning

I have also used the work of Jan Kooiman (2003) on the diversity, complexity and dynamics within governance. The work of these theorists cautions against presenting the two parts of this lecture as 'a stereotyped and demonised past' giving way to 'a visionary and idealised future' (Clarke and Newman, 1997: 49). We must build on the strengths of the sector as well as facing up to where it is going wrong and responding appropriately.

Unprecedented government intervention

The New Labour government has taken post-16 education more seriously than any previous administration by allocating substantial funding, establishing new structures and agencies and creating the first-ever national strategy for skills. The scale of the increased funding can be judged from the grant to the Learning and Skills Council (LSC), which will more than double from £5.5 billion in its first year of operation in 2001–2 to £11.4 billion in 2007–8 (Johnson, 2006, Annex B). Investment in FE colleges has increased by 48 per cent in real terms since 1997 (DfES, 2006a: 14); but investment in schools by 65 per cent (HM Treasury, 2006:131).

Moreover, a torrent of new policy has flooded out from the DfES, including a programme of reform for further education and training, called *Success for All* (DfES, 2002); a *Five Year Strategy for Children and Learners* (DfES, 2004), which was updated in October 2006 (DfES, 2006b); and a White Paper on *Skills: Getting on in business, getting on at work* (DfES, 2005b). A Skills Alliance of government departments and key organisations, representing employers and unions, has been formed to oversee this strategy. A new planning and funding body, the Learning and Skills Council (LSC), was established in 2001 (see Coffield *et al.*, 2005; Hodgson *et al.*, 2005); a new network of Sector Skills Councils began to be formed in 2003 to identify the current and future skill needs of employers; and in 2005 a new Quality Improvement Agency (QIA) was formed to 'drive up' quality throughout the sector.

In addition, the government commissioned two far-ranging reviews. First, a review of the future role of further education colleges by Sir Andrew Foster (2005), and at the same time Lord Leitch (2005) was commissioned by the Chancellor, Gordon Brown, to review future skill needs. Both reports were heavily drawn upon in the White Paper on FE, which ushered in a whole new set of policies, agencies and initiatives, because FE is considered by senior ministers as 'not achieving its full potential as the powerhouse of a high skills economy' (DfES, 2006a: 1). And a Further Education and Training Bill is currently making its way through Parliament.

So the depth, breadth and pace of change coursing through the sector and the unprecedented level of government activity are apparent in:

- a set of new *strategies*
- new stretching *targets*
- a constant stream of *initiatives*[4]
- new *curricula* and *qualifications*
- new *partnerships* between schools and FE colleges
- new types of *institution*, e.g. city academies, skills academies and vocational, specialist schools
- and a new *model* of public service reform, of which more later (PMSU, 2006).

It may seem churlish to criticise what some may see as creative dynamism and others as frenetic hyperactivity, but the very scale and cost of the enterprise prompt serious questions such as:

- Have the new investments and policies resulted in a well-integrated, equitable and inclusive learning *system*? Are the reforms creating the 'radical and enduring change', envisioned by David Blunkett (2000: 1)?
- Are the reforms creating a healthy, innovative and self-confident sector? Is it headed in the right direction?
- Have the main problems facing the sector been acknowledged and are they being tackled?

Current strengths

David Raffe warned against the danger of seeing English post-16 education and training as 'not only distinctive, but distinctively pathological … [where] reform proposals have been dominated by a deficit model' (2002: 11). He suggested an alternative approach which begins by identifying the strengths of the sector and then building on them. He offered the following positive features: institutional flexibility and responsiveness; a tradition of local innovation and second chances; a tradition of pastoral care, and of learning in and through employment with high levels of early career mobility; and young people with a strong sense of agency. I agree with David, and our project suggests further strengths: a deep commitment from tutors to students which is at the core of their professionalism; very high levels of satisfaction among students; meeting the needs of those students who have performed poorly at GCSE and whom no other organisation is keen to teach; the vast range of provision from below Level 1 to Level 5 and for students aged 14 to 99; a steady supply of most of the country's intermediate skills; and the role of adult and community education in strengthening social cohesion. The interim report of the Leitch review of skills in the UK suggested one further strength: 'a strong record of improvement over the past decade' (2005: 1). It went on, however, to warn that 'Even if the Government's current ambitious targets were met' by 2020, 'the UK will continue to be an 'average performer' – positioned, at best, in the middle of the OECD ranking' (Leitch, 2005: 10). In short, these very real strengths and improvements have to be set against a set of long-standing structural, political, theoretical and operational weaknesses.

Current weaknesses

Our research project simultaneously looks down into the sector from the perspectives of senior officials at national and regional levels; and it looks up into the sector from the perspectives of 'front-line' managers, tutors and learners in our 24 learning sites. This scrutiny suggests seven glaring deficiencies:

1 A badly co-ordinated sector, headed in the wrong direction

The White Paper on FE of March 2006 accepted the main recommendation of the Foster Report (2005) and established a new mission for the sector: its 'key strategic role ... is to help people gain the skills and qualifications for employability' (DfES, 2006a: 21). It also argued that the sector should be 'reconfigured' around this mission and claimed that 'this strong focus on economic impact does not come at the expense of social inclusion and equality of opportunity – the two reinforce one another' (DfES, 2006a: 29). Since the publication of the White Paper, however, the main mission for FE is slowly becoming the sole mission, with colleges up and down the country closing courses not linked to it.

Serious and inequitable as that is, a greater error lies in the choice of employability as the core mission, for it is an empty, unsatisfying concept which will sell our people short. For some, such as Jacky Brine, drawing on the work of Ulrich Beck, employability means 'a state of constant becoming', a readiness to be trained and re-trained for whatever types of employment are available, which leaves learners searching for individual solutions to systemic problems (Brine, 2006: 652). In the language of C. Wright Mills, employability turns the public issue of the dearth of good jobs into the private trouble of constant retraining.

Basil Bernstein preferred to criticise what he called the 'jejune concept of trainability', which for him does not create an individual, psychological condition, but a new social identity arising out of a new social order, based on short-term capitalism (Bernstein, 1996: 67). And Richard Sennett has shown how the principle of 'no long term ... corrodes trust, loyalty and mutual commitment' (1998: 24). Employability, then, cannot be the core mission for this crucial sector, because it militates against students understanding or criticising power relations in college or at work or forming a strong vocational identity. The sector needs a different future which gives equal weight to social justice and economic prosperity; and why not, for once, in that order?

Furthermore, within the post-compulsory sector, relations between the key partners are either dysfunctional or disorganised or both. Our earlier reports on the LSC (Coffield *et al.*, 2005; Hodgson *et al.*, 2005) showed how the DfES micromanaged the LSC, which in turn controlled the regional and local LSCs, which then attempted to micromanage the FE colleges and training providers in their locality. After considering the relations between the DfES and the LSC, Foster recommended that their roles should be refined so as 'to lighten the impact of centralised control and monitoring, and to minimise duplication and undue central demands' (2005: 62-3).

Co-ordination between the maintained school sector and the LSS is also poor, as can be seen from what the policy makers themselves call 'the scandal of our high drop-out rate at 16' (DfES, 2004: 71). The OECD has for years been emphasising the extent of that scandal in its annual reports, where it compares internationally the participation rate of 17-year-olds in education or training. The latest report shows that the UK record is worse than that of Belgium, the Czech Republic, Sweden, Japan, Finland, South Korea, Poland, Norway, Germany, France, Austria, Hungary, the Slovak Republic, Ireland, the Netherlands, Switzerland, the USA, Denmark and Australia (OECD, 2006). Part of the problem is that the best resourced routes, which also happen to be the most clearly signposted, are for those students who find learning easiest, while the poorly resourced routes, which are more numerous and more complicated to follow, are for those who find learning difficult.

The official rhetoric talks of 'seamless progression' but every year almost 300,000 fall out of the system at age 16. Part of the explanation is the accountability regime for secondary schools, which pushes teachers to concentrate their efforts on those students who can reach the government-imposed target of five good GCSEs to the detriment of those who cannot. In their effort to push up the 'key marginals' (Hyman, 2005) from D to C grades, teachers, in order to protect themselves, ignore those who are unlikely to reach this level and many then leave school damaged as learners. This is a structural problem of the first importance, which is landed on FE colleges and employers.

The measure of five good passes perpetuates the historic division in English education between O-level sheep and CSE goats, between educating learners and training followers (see Edwards, 1997); it also intensifies the polarisation of performance between highly successful and poorly achieving schools, with 56 per cent of 16-year-olds gaining five good GCSEs, which means that 44 per cent still do not (DfES, 2005c: 14). Five good grades at GCSE have come to be regarded as the measure of success expected of all pupils but, as Peter Mortimore has pointed out, the GCSE 'is not an examination that has been designed for everyone to pass' (2006: 39). We need different measures of school effectiveness and we need to stop the damage done each year to the bottom 44 per cent of each age cohort, who learn that they have failed to reach the minimal standard necessary for employability – and employability is becoming the sole mission of FE.

The priority for policy should be the design of lifelong progression routes which carry students over transitions and on to the completion of courses: participation is no longer sufficient. The Foundation Learning Tier is an important innovation, but, at present, Level 1 and Level 2 students who have left school cannot continue with courses of general education but must choose between the 5,000+ vocational qualifications in the National Qualifications Framework (Foster, 2005: 71); and the information, advice and guidance available to them is 'out of date, fragmented and ill-informed' (2005: 39).

Current policy also tends to concentrate on the learning of young people, but the final report of the Leitch review of skills points out that 'Today, over 70 per cent of our 2020 workforce have already completed their compulsory education' (Leitch, 2006: 1). The further education of adults, employed and unemployed, is the larger and more pressing task.

Further problems are created by the sheer diversity and complexity of the

LSS, as illustrated in Figure 2, which pulls together the institutional architecture in 2005 at a national level, and at one regional and one local level. The diversity of partners is apparent from the need to use more than 20 acronyms, but what is missing is the diversity in values, goals, interests and power. By 'complexity' I mean more than that the sector is difficult to understand or change; I mean it is composed of a number of interrelated sub-systems, each of which is more or less organised or disorganised.

Earlier this year that landscape was 'rationalised', both by government creating a single agency (QIA) for quality improvement, and by organisations such as the LSC creating new Local Partnerships and Economic Development Teams. As Figure 3 demonstrates, however, the result could hardly be described as a slimmed-down sector; in fact, the landscape has become even more crowded as new agencies come into being. Is it any wonder that Ewart Keep (2006) has called state control of this sector 'playing with the biggest train set in the world'? In March 2005 the White Paper on Skills acknowledged that 'there has been concern about the complexity of the organisational landscape', but argued 'To some extent, that complexity is inevitable in such a vast system' (DfES, 2005b Part 2: 69). Inevitability is the first refuge of the lazy fatalist. The landscape urgently needs to be simplified and I shall make some proposals in the final section.[5]

What cannot, however, be captured in two-dimensional diagrams is the third of Jan Kooiman's (2003) three central features of governance: i.e. not only diversity and complexity but dynamics – the innumerable interactions among the partners within the sector, and the pressures for reform from government departments, which result in tensions both between and within organisations. In contrast, Figure 4 attempts to capture something of the 'view from below' in 2006, where the relationships between tutors and learners dominate the scene and only those government initiatives which directly impinge on the lives of learners (e.g. Educational Maintenance Allowances or Skills for Life) are visible to them, whereas organisations like the Regional Development Agency (RDA) or the local LSC, if the acronyms are recognised at all, are opaque abstractions.

Figure 2 The landscape in 2005 of post-16 learning: nationally, regionally and in one locality

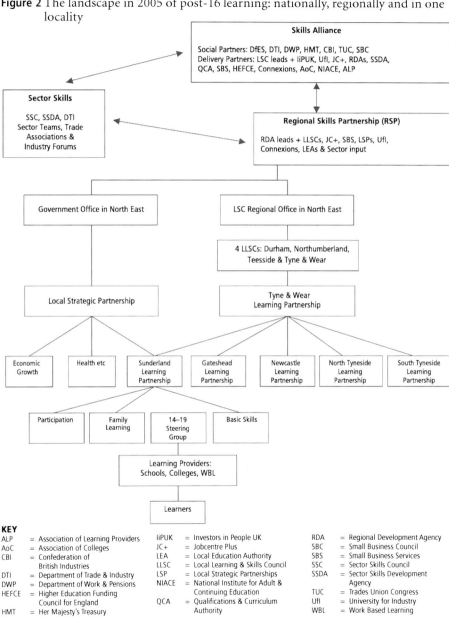

KEY

ALP	= Association of Learning Providers	IiPUK	= Investors in People UK	RDA	= Regional Development Agency
AoC	= Association of Colleges	JC+	= Jobcentre Plus	SBC	= Small Business Council
CBI	= Confederation of British Industries	LEA	= Local Education Authority	SBS	= Small Business Services
		LLSC	= Local Learning & Skills Council	SSC	= Sector Skills Council
DTI	= Department of Trade & Industry	LSP	= Local Strategic Partnerships	SSDA	= Sector Skills Development Agency
DWP	= Department of Work & Pensions	NIACE	= National Institute for Adult & Continuing Education		
HEFCE	= Higher Education Funding Council for England			TUC	= Trades Union Congress
		QCA	= Qualifications & Curriculum Authority	Ufl	= University for Industry
HMT	= Her Majesty's Treasury			WBL	= Work Based Learning

Figure 3 The post-compulsory sector in England in 2006

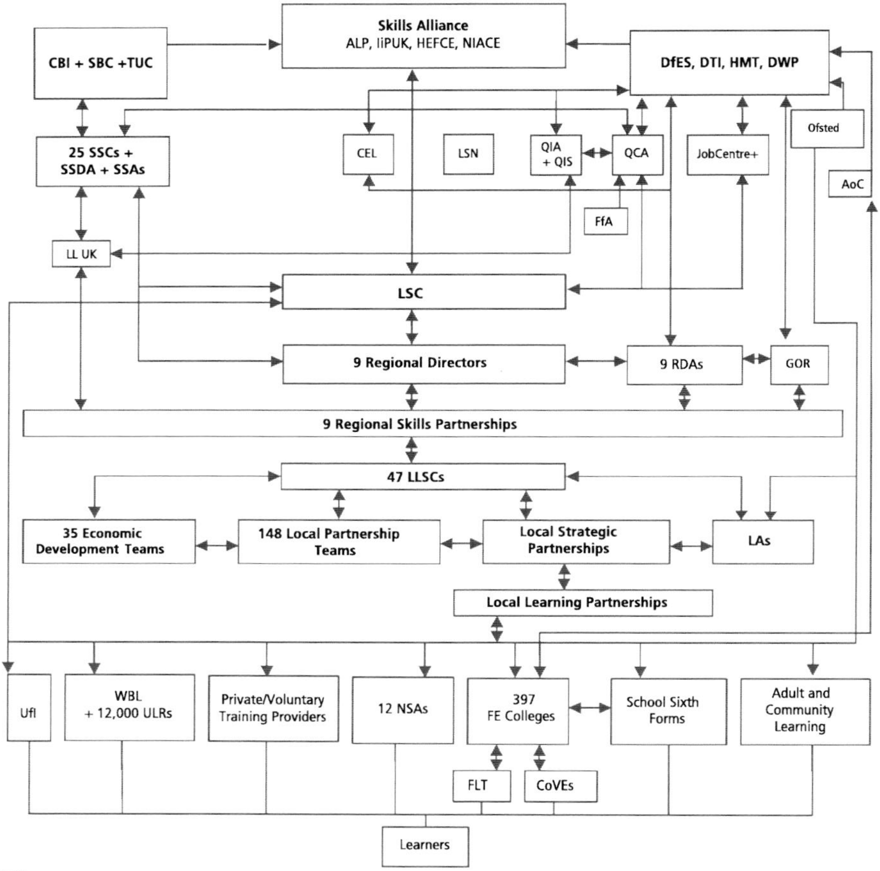

KEY

ALP	= Association of Learning Providers		LSC	= Learning and Skills Council
AoC	= Association for Colleges		LSN	= Learning and Skills Network
CBI	= Confederation of British Industry		NIACE	= National Institute for Adult and Continuing
CEL	= Centre for Excellence in Leadership			Education
CoVEs	= Centres of Vocational Excellence		NSAs	= National Skills Academies
DfES	= Department for Education and Skills		QCA	= Qualifications and Curriculum Authority
DTI	= Department of Trade and Industry		QIA	= Quality Improvement Agency
DWP	= Department of Work and Pensions		QIS	= Quality Improvement Strategy
FE	= Further Education		RDA	= Regional Development Agencies
FfA	= Framework for Achievement		SBC	= Small Business Council
FLT	= Foundation Learning Tiers		SSAs	= Sector Skills Agreements
GOR	= Government Offices in the Regions		SSC	= Sector Skills Council
HEFCE	= Higher Education Funding Council for England		SSDA	= Sector Skills Development Agency
HMT	= Her Majesty's Treasury		TUC	= Trades Union Congress
IiPUK	= Investors in People UK		Ufl	= University for Industry
LA	= Local Authority		ULR	= Union Learning Representative
LLSC	= Local Learning and Skills Council		WBL	= Work Based Learning

14

Figure 4 The post-compulsory sector: the view from below

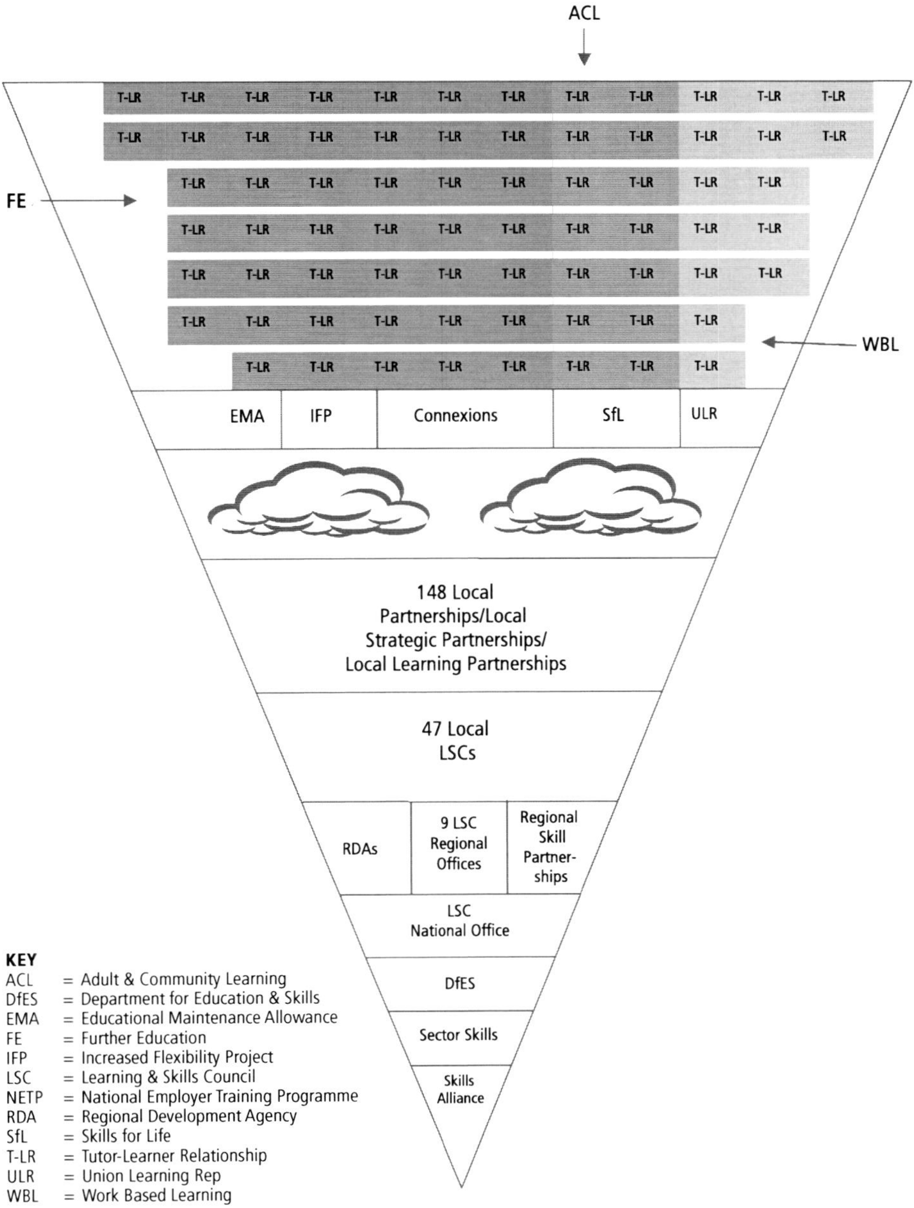

ACL

| T-LR | T-LR | T-LR | T-LR | T-LR | T-LR | T-LR | T-LR | T-LR | T-LR | T-LR | T-LR |
| T-LR | T-LR | T-LR | T-LR | T-LR | T-LR | T-LR | T-LR | T-LR | T-LR | T-LR | T-LR |

FE

	T-LR	T-LR	T-LR	T-LR	T-LR	T-LR	T-LR	T-LR	T-LR	T-LR
	T-LR	T-LR	T-LR	T-LR	T-LR	T-LR	T-LR	T-LR	T-LR	T-LR
	T-LR	T-LR	T-LR	T-LR	T-LR	T-LR	T-LR	T-LR	T-LR	T-LR
	T-LR	T-LR	T-LR	T-LR	T-LR	T-LR	T-LR	T-LR	T-LR
		T-LR	T-LR	T-LR	T-LR	T-LR	T-LR	T-LR	T-LR

WBL

| EMA | IFP | Connexions | SfL | ULR |

148 Local
Partnerships/Local
Strategic Partnerships/
Local Learning Partnerships

47 Local
LSCs

| RDAs | 9 LSC Regional Offices | Regional Skill Partnerships |

LSC
National Office

DfES

Sector Skills

Skills
Alliance

KEY
ACL = Adult & Community Learning
DfES = Department for Education & Skills
EMA = Educational Maintenance Allowance
FE   = Further Education
IFP = Increased Flexibility Project
LSC = Learning & Skills Council
NETP = National Employer Training Programme
RDA = Regional Development Agency
SfL = Skills for Life
T-LR = Tutor-Learner Relationship
ULR = Union Learning Rep
WBL = Work Based Learning

2 Three harmful assumptions

Educational policy continues to be based on three underlying and damaging assumptions: first, that 'our future depends on our skills' (Foster, 2005: 9); second, that in all matters concerning vocational education and the skills strategy it is appropriate 'to put employers in the driving seat' (DfES, 2004: 45); and third, that market competition is essential to make providers efficient and responsive. All three of these assumptions have been roundly criticised for almost 30 years (e.g. Karabel and Halsey, 1977; Coffield, 1999; Bartlett *et al.*, 2000; Wolf, 2002; Ball, 1993; Ball *et al.*, 2000), but they continue to appear in ministerial pronouncements as though they were eternal truths which only a fool would deny. This fool denies all three.

Politicians throughout the developed world have seized upon a debased version of human capital theory to legitimise their conversion of social and economic inequalities into educational problems. Witness Tony Blair, who claimed: 'A country such as Britain in the 21st century will succeed or fail by how it develops its human capital' (2005). This dangerous over-simplification needs to be compared with the Treasury's more sophisticated argument, where skills are only one of the five drivers of productivity, along with investment in physical capital, science and innovation, competition and enterprise (HM Treasury, 2001). In short, we need to ditch 'the belief in a simple, direct relationship between the amount of education in a society and its future growth rate' (Wolf, 2002: 244). Policies based on such a belief raise expectations unreasonably of the likely effects of investment in education on either rectifying unjustifiable inequalities or stimulating economic growth (see Edwards, 2001).

One effect of this concentration on human capital is that education is expected to carry the lion's share of the burden of reform. The government's own figures show that only 'one fifth of the gap [in productivity] with France and Germany is a result of the UK's comparatively poor skills' (Leitch, 2005: 4). So we need to ask Lord Leitch: where are the plans to deal with the factors which are responsible for 80 per cent of that gap? Investment, for example, 'as a proportion of gross domestic product in the UK is, at 17 per cent, the lowest in the G7' (Leitch, 2005: 25). Moreover, the economic returns to investment in qualifications are declining, as more and more young people graduate and face competition from well-educated and professionally trained graduates from Poland, India and China.

As to the second assumption, the history of the repeated attempts by governments of different political complexions to give employers the leading role in developing new policy for the sector is one long story of spurned advances. The previous Secretary of State, Ruth Kelly, described their uneasy relationship thus: 'In the past, Government has let down employers when it has tried to guess what different sectors need. But equally, employers have been guilty of watching Government initiatives from the sidelines and expressing disappointment when they inevitably land wide of the mark' (2005a). Leaving aside the admission that governmental initiatives 'inevitably' fail, I would argue that the behaviour of employers is better interpreted as a lack of interest in the roles which government continually proposes for them. Kelly, in her White Paper on 14–19-year-olds, underlined her determination 'to put employers in the driving seat, so that they will have a key role in determining what the "lines of learning" should be and in deciding in detail what the Diplomas should contain' (DfES, 2005a: 45). Employers do not want this responsibility.

Should they, however, have been offered such a privileged position over both the vocational curriculum and the national strategy for skills? Such a commanding role may very well damage the government's attempt to form a new Skills Alliance, which in its own words is meant to be 'a new social partnership for skills' (DfES, 2003: 100). The relationship between government and employers needs to be rethought, with the government being prepared to take the leading role on behalf of the whole community. Instead of offering business and industrial leaders roles they do not want, government needs to acknowledge the continuing failures caused by our de-regulated labour market, and move away from the voluntary organisation of training by challenging those employers who do not train their own workers (see Coffield, 2004).

The third harmful assumption is that the introduction of market forces into public services will guarantee efficiency, responsiveness and greater choice for users; but the government's determination to create more diversity is a euphemism for introducing a new hierarchy among schools. Moreover, 'the key trope for all social policy is the private firm, which is presented as the model of effectiveness' (Ball, 2005). The final report of the Leitch review of skills refers to comparative research on management in the USA, UK, France and Germany, which showed 'UK firms to be the most poorly managed' (2006: 52).

What is so harmful about these propositions is that they are advanced without any empirical evidence to support them and often in the teeth of findings which flatly contradict them. What is being forgotten is that historically public services were provided to overcome injustices created by free markets, so considerations of equity should take precedence over economic factors such as efficiency. And yet, exactly the opposite happens in the latest publications on the pursuit of excellence from the LSC (2006a, 2006b) and the QIA (2006). As James C. Scott argues, 'in markets, money talks, not people' (1998: 8).

Ewart Keep has shown how these ideological assumptions and others are part of a 'shared policy narrative … that binds the system together and helps establish the limits for public debate about vocational education and training along lines determined by ministers and senior civil servants' (forthcoming: 7). There is a word in English for a set of passionately held beliefs which are impervious to doubt, argument or evidence. That word is fundamentalism.

3 The proliferation of policy

Peter Hyman switched from writing speeches for Tony Blair in Number 10 to working in an inner-city school in London, and witnessed in his former post 'the tyranny of momentum politics at first hand.… Constant … activity to show a department was serious about change … conspired to make the lives of frontline staff more frustrating and more difficult' (2005: 272). In order to prevent the media running hostile stories, Number 10 felt it had to seize the headlines every day: 'Because we wanted to show momentum, departments and Number 10 were constantly looking for things to announce' (2005: 269). The inconsistencies, confusions and illogicalities in the Schools White Paper, *Higher Standards, Better Schools for All* (DfES, 2005c) suggest that it is a prime example of momentum and presidential politics, where policy-making has become over-centralised and confrontational (see Eagle, 2006).

Rather than awaiting the verdict of evaluations, the ministerial response to the failure of previous policy tends to be more policy; but the sheer volume of policy, and the tensions created by conflicts within policy now constitute one of the main barriers to progress. 'Between 1997 and the general election of 2005 there were eight Acts of Parliament on education issues' (House of Commons Education and Skills Committee, 2006: 6). To change a famous remark of Dennis Potter's: 'For me, policy is not the bandage, it's the wound'. The post-compulsory sector is currently saturated with policies which deflect resources and energies from the central tasks of teaching and learning. Government ministers do not need to be persuaded of this argument; it is their practice which needs to change. Witness Charles Clarke's admission: '[Education reform] depends on Ministers like me holding our nerve and being able to resist the lure of the next initiative in favour of a system that drives its own improvement more and more' (2004: 5). He did not resist; the flood of initiatives has continued unabated.

John Clarke and Janet Newman make two incisive comments about such policy proliferation. First, it 'stems from a government seeking to control an unstable field of policy delivery in which … problems repeatedly refuse to be depoliticised and so require an ever-increasing set of policy interventions' (1997: 145). Second, policy vacuums emerge in the space between endless policy initiatives and the lack of coherence between them. They provide practitioners with some 'elbow room' to adapt rather than apply policy, and with some discursive space for debating change and reshaping it in ways more in keeping with their professional values and the needs of their students.

4 Over-regulation

Given the barrage of criticism that has been levelled at the heavy-handed regulatory regimes imposed by government on the public services (e.g. Power, 1997; Ball, 2003; Newman, 2001; O'Neil, 2002), one might have hoped that lessons would have been learned and that the high point of excessive regulation would have passed by now. Certainly, the language of official texts has altered and some of the terminology of the leading critics has been incorporated into official rhetoric. For instance, the LSC's *Agenda for Change* asserted that 'rigorous, comprehensive **self-assessment** is at the heart of organisational development and an essential tool for managing change' (2005b: 6, original emphasis). Similarly, the White Paper on 14–19 Education and Skills argued that the new 'intelligent accountability framework … should mobilise and motivate institutions' (2005: 81–2). The new wording is, I think, a tribute to the philosopher Onora O'Neil, who in her Reith Lectures argued that: 'If we want greater accountability without damaging professional performance we need intelligent accountability', which she defined as requiring 'more attention to good governance and fewer fantasies about total control. Good governance is possible only if institutions are allowed some margin for self-governance' (2002, Lecture 3, 5).

Whether these official protestations about a change of heart will be borne out in practice only time will tell, but already the signs are not good. The LSC's *Framework for Excellence* (2006b), for instance, proposes seven new 'key performance indicators', but each of these is divided into several constituent measures, making up a minimum of 27 new indicators in all (see Table 1). And yet the LSC believes the new regulatory framework will require 'the minimum of additional work' (ibid.: 11). It would be laughable if it were not so serious.

What we are witnessing is an accountability framework, whose measures become steadily more numerous and, at the same time, ever more stretching, robust, tough, and challenging, being accommodated and normalised, as professionals develop ever more creative methods of coping. Ministers are likely to run out of adjectives to describe the intensifying rigour of their approach before professionals run out of ingenious methods of complying.

Table 1 Table of Measures

Key Performance Indicator	Possible basis for the constituent measures	Mapping to the CIF
Delivery against plan	Assessment of the overall performance against plan will be based on the Summary Statement of Activity together with the agreed improvement indicators. It will incorporate the Provision Matrix.	Question 5
Responsiveness to learners	The composite will involve self-assessment, but will probably include an analysis of: • learner satisfaction • learner destination and progression • college's or provider's equality and diversity impact measures.	Questions 3 and 4
Responsiveness to employers	This will be a composite indicator that will require judgements against criteria to be made. An initial indicator can be developed from quantitative indicators together with qualitative data such as accreditation to the new standard (building on CoVE and the Quality Mark). The resultant indicator will have to be mission-specific.	Question 3
Quality of provision	The primary component will be Ofsted judgement and the second component will be the institution's self-assessment against the CIF validated by peer review, annual assessment visits and inspection.	Questions 2, 3 and 4
Quality of outcomes	A quantified assessment of learner outcome is required. It is likely that the assessment will be based around the New Measures of Success currently being introduced.	Question 1
Financial health	Financial health is being revised to focus on three key measures: • solvency (current ratio) • sustainability (margin) • status (net worth). Each of these measures will be benchmarked and allow drill-down to further financial and efficiency analyses.	Question 5
Financial control	The financial control measure will be based on the evidence of auditors and other finance-based reviews of colleges and providers. It will pick up qualitative factors in financial management that are not conveyed by the numbers in the financial health measure, for example the institution's soundness of internal control, regularity and propriety in use of LSC funds, and quality of deployment of financial resources in achieving the college's or provider's objectives.	Question 5

Source: LSC (2006b) *Framework for Excellence*, p16

Governments throughout the western world currently employ policy 'instruments', which vary from being coercive to enabling, in their attempts to shape public services. These 'new technologies of power', as Newman called them (2005: 12), are not, however, nearly as powerful as those who wield them desire. For example, the percentage of 16-year-olds in full-time learning (75.4 per cent) has been stuck on a plateau for almost 10 years.

Moreover, policy 'drivers' suggest a model of change which is crudely mechanical rather than interactive and sensitive. The theory and the language which governments and policy makers currently employ to describe the management of change in education and in the public services more generally are not suited to the task. For example, neither the curriculum nor targets can be 'delivered' as though they were the post or pizzas. 'Levers', 'drivers' and 'steering mechanisms' suggest that control can be exercised mechanically over fixed objects by applying the appropriate 'tool': but talk of 'toolboxes' and 'tools for the job' suggest that policy can be 'implemented' as easily as pulling the right levers. Both the language and the model of change are inappropriate and need to be replaced.

The current fashion for over-regulation has one further, and hopefully fatal, weakness: the very countries whose higher productivity we are seeking to emulate achieve 'a high level of quality and standing without the heavy central control and complex accountability arrangements operating in our FE system' (Foster, 2005: 97). The English sector was compared by Sir Andrew Foster and his advisory group with its equivalent in the United States, Denmark, Australia, the Netherlands and Ontario, and the key difference was the lack of trust in professionals by English politicians and policy makers. As a Scandinavian commentator phrased it: 'The English are wasting millions trying to prove they are getting value for money'. One need only cross the border into Scotland or Wales to appreciate how extreme social policy in England has become.

5 Lack of democratic accountability

Over many decades, and under both Conservative and Labour administrations, the powers of local government have been gradually whittled away.[6] The upshot is what Geoff Mulgan has called the great irony of English local government: 'it's neither very local, nor much like government' (2006: 10).

The same period has also seen an explosion in the number of local partnerships involving the public, private and voluntary sectors, e.g. local strategic partnerships and local learning partnerships, whose decisions are not subject to local political accountability.[7] The current shape of local governance can be summarised as *central command and local delivery*, a relationship explained more fully by Janet Newman as follows: 'Local authorities were required to act as the agents through which a set of prescriptive government policies would be delivered, with little scope to shape or retain local diversity' (2001: 77).

The rhetoric of government now favours 'double devolution', whereby power is to be passed down apparently not only from the centre to local government, but also from cities and counties to neighbourhoods and communities. Their predominant practice since 1997, however, has been just as remorselessly to increase central control because of a basic distrust of local government, which is considered to be 'incompetent and parochial, mediocre and stagnant' (Mulgan, 2006: 8). The recent White Paper on Local Government admits that there are currently 600 separate elements in the performance management of local by central government, and that '80% of reporting [is] focused on meeting top-down requirements' (Department for Communities and Local Government (DCLG), 2006: 117). The Foreword by the Prime Minister contains no hint of an apology for such self-indulgent and intemperate centralism, but he has the gall to claim he now wants 'to see local authorities rising to the challenge of leading their areas' (DCLG, 2006 : 3). Can the proposed reform of local government, however, break out of the dilemma whereby central government will not devolve power until local government becomes more accountable and competent while local government claims it cannot become more accountable and competent without greater devolution?

In all these discussions there is little discussion of accountability to the citizens who provide the money. In the LSS, for instance, the Chair and Chief Executive of the LSC, the members of its National Council, its Adult Learning Committee and its Young People's Learning Committee and the council members of the 47 local LSCs are all appointed by the Secretary of State. The same is true of the Sector Skills Development Agency, which is not so much a voice of the employers as an agent of the DfES. Hence Skelcher (1998) talked of 'the Appointed State', where governance is based on appointed rather than elected bodies. In the financial year 2004–5, the LSC devoted only 1.29 per cent of its huge budget to the Local Initiatives Fund (LSC, 2005a).

The contradiction in policy is at its most acute in this area, as the White Paper promises 'to deliver a step change in promoting [local] cohesion' (DCLG, 2006: 12), while the Prime Minister's Strategy Unit imposes city academies on town halls. In one of our research areas, the main players in 14–19 education formed a successful learning partnership centred on a shared educational value, namely, a commitment to raise the attainment of *all* young people in the area and not just that of a minority. That common stance brought them into direct conflict with national educational policy, as advanced by Number 10, which insisted on the establishment of a city academy and threatened to withdraw funds for the renovation of school buildings if its wishes were not complied with. The cohesion of local communities is weakened by government, which then introduces new measures to rectify the problems it has caused.

If 'double devolution' is to become more than a fashionable slogan, it will need to be defined as the devolution of substantial power and resources and perhaps even the right to raise local taxes. When FE colleges are given discretionary control of, say, 20 per cent of their core budget, we shall know the government is serious about localism (see NIACE, 2005: 4).

6 'Upskilling and reskilling the workforce'

The language and the thinking behind this phrase are ugly, and come from government publications where parents, students or employers are placed 'in the driving seat' and given the key role in reform. By implication, those who are permanently parked in the back seat are the professionals. The image of the ideal practitioner in the LSS conveyed by the official texts is of a technician or government agent who is regularly upgraded in order to implement without question the latest government initiative, who 'personalises' the learning of all his or her students, while simultaneously responding to the ever-changing, short-term needs of local employers. The White Paper on 14–19 summed up this attitude in a chilling phrase: 'We will ensure that the workforce can implement what they are asked to do' (DfES, 2005a: 25). The government's aim is a workforce which passively receives the training thought appropriate for it rather than a profession of experts capable of self-improvement. The teaching profession is being re-formed, as Geoff Whitty argued, with teachers being restricted to 'craft skills rather than professional understanding' (1997: 304). The aim appears to be initiatives which are 'professional-proof', i.e. immune from teachers' innovation, incompetence or subversion.

The Prime Minister's Strategy Unit has also published a new model of public sector reform which consists of four elements, each of which is intended to exert pressure for change: [8]

- top-down performance management, e.g. targets, standards, inspection;
- market incentives, e.g. competition and contestability;
- users shaping the sector from below, e.g. so-called 'choice and voice';
- increasing the capacity of organisations and the capability of 'the workforce' (see Figure 5).

This model will bear down hard upon the staff, who will have to contend with pressures coming at them from above, below and from both sides. And yet their experiences, concerns and innovative ideas are conspicuously absent from

Figure 5 Government model of public service reform

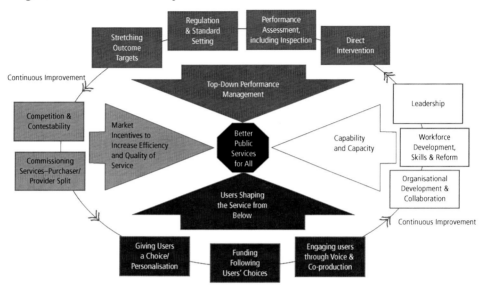

the model, which is a closed system. It claims to have embedded incentives for continuous improvement and innovation, but instead treats 'the workforce' as another lever to be pulled. In short, professionals in the LSS are neither equal nor full partners in reform, they are the *target* of reform (see Figure 6).

What is missing from this approach are two ingredients of success. First, Seymour Sarason (1990) explained the predictable failure of all educational reform as follows: tutors cannot create and sustain the conditions for their students to become lifelong learners, if those conditions do not exist for the tutors. Those conditions currently do not exist in the sector. Just look at the libraries in FE colleges compared with those in HE; they are living proof of generations of under-funding.

Second, there is no systematic feedback loop (or set of loops) whereby managers and tutors can report back to policy makers on the strengths and weaknesses of the reforms.[9] Traffic in educational policy remains strictly one-way.[10] Tutors, managers and LSC staff need to be involved at all stages in the

Figure 6 Impact of government reform on staff

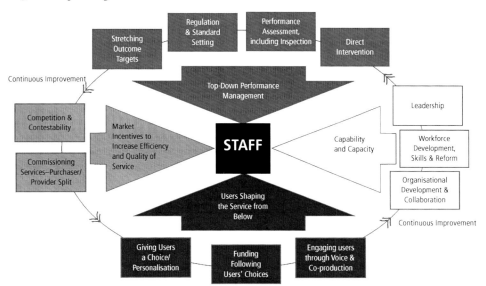

development, enactment, evaluation and re-design of policy, but the separation of policy and 'delivery' has made it far more difficult to involve in policy-making the very people who know most about the struggle to make sense of the constant through-put of new policies and initiatives.

7 The hole in the heart of the sector

Shortly after coming to power in 1997, the New Labour government issued a Green Paper, *The Learning Age* (DFEE, 1998), which claimed to place learners at the heart of the sector. Five years later this had changed to 'putting Teaching, Training and Learning at the heart of what we do' (DfES, 2002: 29), which is a distinct improvement. In all the pelting torrent of official documents which have flooded the sector since 1997, there is, however, one significant silence: there is no discussion, and not even a definition, of the central concept of learning, although the word 'learning' is pervasive in such texts and deliberately used in preference to the term 'education'.[11] And yet the whole programme of reform is dependent on some unstated notion of what constitutes learning and, especially, how we become better at learning. The implicit model is a simple input–output one; and government concern to improve the quality of everyone's learning has not spilled over into an interest in learning itself. No learning society is likely ever to be created in the UK or anywhere else without an appropriate theory (or theories) of learning.

Let me briefly sum up at this point. Any one of the seven weaknesses identified above would have been serious; together they point to a sector which, for all its strengths and achievements, is also in deep trouble, with senior ministers impatiently goading it to go faster down the wrong road. I am keen not to be misunderstood on this point. I am *not* arguing that what we are witnessing is endless change without progress. There *has been* progress on a large number of fronts; I have time to mention only one: the quantity and quality of basic-skills training has improved substantially in recent years. My case is that we are experiencing permanent revolution without the most fundamental problems being tackled.

The official narrative would have us believe that ministers pull 'levers' (e.g. funding, planning, targets, inspection and initiatives) to 'drive' the system. But one participant at one of our research seminars identified what really animates this sector – fear. Number 10 Downing Street and the Treasury instruct ministers within the DfES, who exert pressure on DfES officials, who then micromanage the LSC, who in turn use inspection reports, performance management and contestability to frighten colleges, who have to harry their own tutors in order to survive. An education sector run on fear, however, is a contradiction in terms and it will, given time, crumble from within like the Soviet Union. In the meantime it is damaging those working within it. When the sector is periodically restructured, the official euphemism talks of 'transaction costs', which refer to redundancy payments and all the other expenses involved in closing down one agency and establishing another. What cannot be calculated and what is not discussed are the *human* costs: the careers broken, the people harmed and the able staff who leave the profession.

Towards a learning system?

What follows is the contribution of one individual and is therefore limited, tentative and open to criticism and improvement. I am here exercising my democratic right to principled, constructive dissent by 'gathering our resources for a journey of hope' (Williams, 1983: 268).

A new settlement

First, we need nothing less than a new settlement between government, officials, employers, researchers and professionals. Sir Andrew Foster was right to argue that, as the architect of education, 'DfES should provide a coherent and managed framework spanning schools, FE and HE' (2005: 7). Certainly, we should learn to work across the sectors, and we also need 'a new, open and trust-based relationship between LSC and DfES' (2005: 80), but something more fundamental must come first.

We need a change in the culture of government at the highest level, because those who demand continuous change of others are exactly those in most need of changing their own practices. There are, in other words, demands for reform that we should make *of* government as well as receiving demands *from* it. The first requisite of a learning system is a government which shows itself capable of learning, of having at times the confidence to be uncertain or to admit it was wrong, and which acts as a role model for all the organisations, professionals and students within the system. Instead, since 1979 we have had governments untroubled by doubt, counter-argument or research, who feel passionately about each and every one of their projects, however ill-considered, and who ignore or ridicule constructive criticism rather than learning from it.

David Blunkett, in his recently published account of his time in office, commented as follows about a meeting held in this building: 'If the Institute of Education wanted to influence me and my ministers they had certainly gone entirely the wrong way about it. I wasn't prepared even to countenance listening to what they had to say' (2006: 109). Irrespective of what happened that evening in 1999, and I was not present, these comments by a Secretary of State for Education reek not only of the arrogance of power but of a determination *not* to learn. Another example. Estelle Morris at the BERA conference in September 2006 admitted that the government changed within one week the literacy strategy, which had taken years to construct, in favour of synthetic phonics because of a campaign in the *Daily Mail*. So, clearly it is not researchers who have influence with ministers but the tabloids.

Luckily, there are some optimistic signs. The LSC in its 'agenda for change' (2005b) offers a more open, self-critical approach, based on dialogue and discussion with its partners.[12] Gordon Brown has also argued: 'To build trust, we must also listen more, hear more and learn more' (2006). Yes, but it is the behaviour of ministers which needs to change.

The rapidity with which ministers and civil servants are reshuffled also adversely affects all government departments and not just education, as Chris Mullin MP has pointed out.[13] There have been, for example, seven Ministers for Lifelong Learning since 1997;[14] and in the Cabinet reshuffle of April 2006 Douglas Alexander became the seventh Minister of Transport in nine years and John Reid took up his ninth post in nine years. The Prime Minister apparently thinks that Dr John Reid is fit for nine purposes; funny, I can only think of one. Such constant movement disrupts working relationships, prevents the deep understanding of the challenges faced by particular ministries and promotes short-term thinking and action. We must also have a decisive break with momentum and presidential politics and the culture of constant interference and endless initiatives, tied to ministerial careers. This government's tragic flaw has been to imagine that such a massive, diverse and dynamic sector could be micromanaged from 10 Downing Street.

The institutional architecture also needs rationalisation. The LSC should be combined with the SSDA (see EEF, 2006), and the 47 sub-regional offices of the LSC should be quietly abandoned. Some amalgamation also needs to take place between the regional LSCs, the RDAs, and the Regional Skills Partnerships to strengthen and streamline regional governance. At local level, the local strategic partnerships should absorb both the LSC partnership teams and the local learning partnerships. And the proliferation of new bodies needs to stop.

The politicians of all parties also need a new story to tell. An increasingly sophisticated electorate deserves better than the insulting rhetoric to the effect that education on its own can create economic prosperity and social justice. Instead we want to hear how education will become part of a co-ordinated strategy of social, economic and fiscal policies to tackle deep-rooted inequalities.

The final report of the Leitch review of skills was published hours before this inaugural lecture was delivered in December 2006. It claims to have set out 'a radical and compelling vision' (2006: 25); in my view, the report is timid, unconvincing and blinkered. The review is an uncritical hymn of praise to 'economically valuable skills'; and, three times without any supporting evidence, it claims that 'where skills were once a key driver of prosperity and fairness, they are now *the* key driver' (2006: 9, original emphasis). It rightly concludes, however, that 'the UK's skill base remains mediocre by international standards' and, more contentiously, that 'delivering a fully demand-led system is the only [sic] way to ensure that the UK achieves world class skills' (2006: 10 and 74).

The powers of employers are to be extended yet again (e.g. control over all vocational qualifications), but the report fails to argue for a complementary extension of their responsibilities; for instance, statutory time off for training for all employees, such as Swedish workers have enjoyed since 1972. The report is also silent about introducing the *right* of all citizens to lifelong learning, just like their right to pensions or social security. Instead, employers are to be encouraged 'to voluntarily commit to train all eligible employees up to Level 2' (4). In sum, the Leitch review creates a sense of urgency about Britain's comparatively poor performance in education, training and productivity, but then ducks the challenge of standing up to the politicians and the employers.

Social partnership

Part of the new settlement must be a re-ordering of the relationship between the government and employers, because the policy of voluntarism with regard to industrial training, which has been tried for over 30 years, has failed (see Coffield, 1992). If it had succeeded, we would not need a report from Lord Leitch. The New Labour administrations since 1997 have enforced statutory change upon all the public services, but have relied on ineffective exhortations with employers.

Our data provide convincing evidence of regulation which has led to a demand for training where employees, employers and customers all benefit. For instance, the Care Standards Act of 2000 now stipulates that all care workers must be trained to Level 2. Students have come forward in increasing numbers to be trained because the attractiveness and status of care work have been raised. Similarly, the street cleaners we interviewed, some of whom had not had a day's training in 20 years of employment, are now obliged to take an NVQ in order to meet Health and Safety requirements. Such regulation of the market by means of licences to practise could act as a model for increasing demand for training in other sectors, provided that employers and learners are prepared to pay where appropriate.

The main difference, however, between post-16 education in England and the rest of Europe is that we lack the close involvement of all the social partners (government, employers, trade unions, voluntary and community organisations and locally elected representatives) in a forum where consensus is formed on, for instance, the skills, qualifications and training needed to respond to changes in the labour market. Business and education need to work more closely together than ever before, but in a relationship where the private sector is prepared to learn from the public sector as well as vice versa. So far partnerships between business and education have been subjected to constant reorganisation, short-term funding and uncoordinated policy.

Mature self-regulation

The LSC wishes to introduce 'a rigorous and robust self-assessment process' (2006a: 7), but who is to decide whether it is sufficiently rigorous and robust? The answer is more likely to be Ofsted than the colleges themselves or their peers, i.e. a centrally controlled form of self-assessment will be introduced. MPs, let us remember, are in favour of self-regulation to the extent of fixing their own salaries, expenses and pensions.

I support the move towards mature self-regulation, by which I mean peer assessment, greater professional autonomy (e.g. 3-year rather than 1-year plans and budgets), inspection linked to improvement and local networks of collaborative rather than competing institutions. The case for a far greater measure of autonomy was well made by O'Neil: 'If we want a culture of public service, professionals and public servants must in the end be free to serve the public rather than their paymasters' (2002, Lecture 3: 5). The public good will not be served, however, by independent institutions pursuing their own self-interest; institutional autonomy has to be tempered by the need for all educational institutions in an area to work together as part of one system (see Glatter, 2003).

If, however, the technologies of control are becoming ever more unforgiving, how will a new culture of mature self-regulation ever get off the ground? In the short term, targets are being met and inspection scores improved, but it may be at the long-term expense of the capacity for self-improving institutions which are democratic and innovative.

There is also an urgent need to slow the pace of change, but, according to Blair, Brown and Kelly in their Foreword to the White Paper on FE, 'Evolutionary and incremental change will not be enough. We need fundamental reform' (DfES, 2006a: 2). The timescales of politicians are out of 'sync' with those of practitioners and researchers. Speed is both exhilarating and essential for politicians, faced with an election every four years, but disorienting for practitioners, who need to create a sense of order and continuity for their students. Researchers also know from harsh experience that when trying to improve learning in classrooms and institutions, never mind a whole sector, 'changes are likely to be small and gradual (incrementalism) rather than sudden and discontinuous' (Scott, 1998: 332).

Local learning systems

A new geography of power is slowly being constructed. Since 1997, measures supporting both devolution and centralisation have been pursued in government policy.[15] Within the LSC, responsibilities and funding have been transferred from the 47 local offices to nine regional offices and at the same time the LSC is being re-organised into 148 local partnership teams. So what we are witnessing is a complex redistribution of power and resources between different levels of governance rather than a simple transfer to or from the centre. In the words of Stephen Ball, 'Arguably what we are now seeing is more localism *and* more centralisation' (2005: 218, original emphasis). I would add: *and* more regionalisation,[16] despite the overwhelming rejection of a directly elected Regional Assembly by voters in the North East.[17] The critical fact here, however, is that neither the LSC nor the RDAs have a democratic mandate to bring about change. A further problem concerns the drawing of boundaries in ways which make full use of local knowledge, while at the same time identifying areas with sufficient power and resources to effect change.

This is not the place to discuss the detailed reforms needed in the power relationships between central, regional and local government. Instead, I shall suggest the following minimal conditions as necessary for effective, equitable and inclusive local learning systems:

- We need to acknowledge the primacy of local knowledge and informal relationships. There is no substitute for fine-grained knowledge of local areas and institutions (their history and traditions, geography, culture and performance) and of local labour markets (e.g. levels of skill and productivity). National policy should be shaped to fit local needs, values and aspirations.[18]
- In order to re-introduce cohesion and trust, the relationship between all the social and economic partners should be one of

co-operation, with each partner having clearly defined roles and responsibilities and a formal duty to co-operate. One democratically accountable organisation, the Local Authority, should be given the power and responsibility to form local plans, agreed by all the main players, and by local MPs and councillors, to whom the LSC and RDAs should also be accountable on a regular basis. Local Authorities, as we have known them, however, are not up to this task, which will require the active participation of citizens in decision and policy-making (see Lowndes *et al.*, 2006).

- Governance and accountability should be organised nationally and regionally to ensure a fair distribution of resources in order to reduce unjustifiable inequalities.
- The central principle of local partnerships should be a commitment to raising the education and training level of *all* people in the area and not that of a minority: and the planning and funding of all provision should be based on this principle. Providers within an area should be held jointly responsible for local levels of participation and achievement (see Stanton and Fletcher, 2006).
- Funding should be longer term (a minimum of three years), stable and flexible, with greater local discretion to stimulate innovation. Institutions should be expected to work with one, and only one, financial regime which is agreed nationally and regionally among the main players.
- This sector, for all the massive injection of extra funds since 1997, remains seriously underfunded. Sufficient, additional funds are needed to break the inverse law of education, whereby those most in need of high-quality education are least likely to get it. Funding, for example, on Level 1 and 2 students should rise to equal that spent on higher-education students. Contrary to the claim in the title of the Green Paper that *Every Child*

Matters (HM Treasury, 2003), the existing pattern of funding shows that some children, young people and adults matter far more than others. We are currently providing second-class funding for working-class people in institutions which have been under-resourced for generations.

Staff as full, equal partners with a different mission

It is all very well for Sir Andrew Foster to claim that the sector needs 'a purposeful, skilled, professional and inspiring workforce' (2005: 10), but he was silent about the gap which exists between the funding of staff and students in FE colleges and schools (Fletcher and Owen, 2005). The FE White Paper proposes to narrow but not to close this funding gap: 'When resources allow, further steps will be taken' (DfES, 2006a: 68). This is a serious political misjudgement which undermines the government offer of a 'new relationship' with the colleges: this genuine grievance will fester until 'comparable learning is funded at a comparable rate' (ibid.). It will also make it more difficult for the sector to attract new staff.[19] If the current Secretary of State is looking for a quick way of winning over the staff in FE colleges, he should persuade the Treasury to close this gap now.

For some years, the identification and dissemination of 'good practice' has been a central part of the government's reform strategy. 'Good practice', however, is apparently no longer good enough, nor is 'best practice'. The sector is charged, in the FE White Paper, with 'ensuring that the quality of teaching and learning is uniformly excellent' and has been warned that the government will take 'decisive action to eliminate failure' (DfES, 2006a: 18, 55). What next? A demand for ubiquitous perfection? Well, if politicians and the Cabinet can so easily reach and maintain that standard, why should it not be attained by all staff and students?

The QIA has recently offered a definition of excellence: 'We believe that excellence means developing, maintaining and delivering to the highest standards of responsiveness, effectiveness and efficiency' (QIA, 2006: 9).

Two problems. First, *what* is to be developed, maintained and delivered to the highest standards? The new Renault Clio? The morning papers? Creationism? Second, standards are to be judged by the three criteria of responsiveness, effectiveness and efficiency, but equity is not one of the key criteria.

The central role for the sector should, in my view, be improving the quality of teaching and learning in general, vocational and adult education. I deliberately use the term education, unlike the DfES, which in the most recent version of its five-year strategy refers only to 'adult skills' (DfES, 2006b: 20). In short, the government has a strategy for skills, but not one for lifelong learning. DfES now stands for the Department for Employability Skills; education for that half of the population not going on to HE is quietly being dropped.

The most significant finding in our data, in all three types of settings, is that the relationship between the tutor and students is the heart and soul of the job. If improving teaching and learning were to be acknowledged as the core business, then let me suggest what should result. For example, senior management (apart from financial directors, obviously) in schools and colleges should teach, in order to demonstrate its over-riding importance. They are, after all, educational leaders first and business leaders second. Moreover, improving teaching and learning is a collective responsibility which requires an institutional response (see Grubb, 1999). One way to improve the quality of teaching and learning would be to give tutors an entitlement to sabbatical leave, reduce the number of their teaching hours per week to, say, 21, and involve them instead in quality circles, peer observations, and discussions on the latest research into pedagogy. Written policies on teaching and learning need to go way beyond administrative details and offer an explicit model of learning and of change; and be able to show how both are used to make students, tutors, the senior management team and the institution itself better at learning in a person-centred learning community (see Fielding, 2006). A useful set of 'principles of procedure for improving learning' in FE has also been produced by Hodkinson *et al.* (2006).

Although I have argued for staff in the sector to be made full and equal partners in the formation, enactment, evaluation and re-design of policy, I do not idealise them all as heroic, stressed, under-paid and long-suffering reformers. There is a small number of public-service workers who need to be reminded that they are supposed to be offering the public a service. We do not need, however, a formidable battery of regulatory measures to deal with this minor problem. In over 40 years of work in education I cannot recall a government that was able to engage the goodwill and creativity of the teaching profession.

Final comments

I have now worked in England for over 30 years and I have internalised the most important value in English society: 'don't rock the boat'. The captain has, however, transferred his children to a voluntary-aided boat, he has ordered full speed ahead to what I am convinced is an iceberg and he refuses to change course. Is it not just common sense to raise a warning shout? I do not want to rock or capsize the boat because my family, my kids Emma and Tom, and your kids too, we are all in the same boat. I want to steer it out of harm's way. It is this government's intransigence which is putting their futures at risk.

This government has taken the sector more seriously than any previous administration. It has allocated substantial new funding; it has established new structures, agencies and initiatives. Its approach has also chalked up some substantial achievements which deserve to be celebrated, e.g. more than 1.25 million people have improved their basic literacy, numeracy and language skills. The diligence, inventiveness and commitment of ministers cannot be faulted; it is their judgement, their culture, and their failure to act on the main problems which I am questioning here.

After nine years of constant reform,[20] the sector is still inchoate, over-centralised, democratically unaccountable, unequal, woefully under-researched and without robust data for decision-making.[21] The skills strategy is also based on some ill-founded assumptions that need to be re-thought and replaced. As the impatience of ministers has grown with what they see as the slow rate of progress, so their interventions have become more frequent, more hectoring and more controlling. Within the next twelve months I expect a college of further education to be closed '*pour encourager les autres*'. This repeated cycle of unrealistic expectations and short-term punitive interventions is a recipe for long-term failure.

The sector is now weighed down by layer upon layer of policy, some well-thought out, others ill-considered; some still in place, others abandoned. Most create new responsibilities, but responsibilities are never shed; some contain not only inconsistent but irreconcilable strategies to be run simultaneously; and some move power to the centre, some to the region and some to the locality. The upshot is a curious mixture of advances (e.g. a new, more appropriate shape for the LSC) and of regressions (e.g. the growing number of schools outwith local democratic accountability). We are witnessing the main tensions within the sector being played out in the professional lives of staff, i.e. those between competition and collaboration, between standardisation and innovation, between centralisation and local flexibility, between enabling and controlling strategies, and between long-term sustainability and short-term goals and targets.

The challenges of creating radical and enduring reform have been seriously underestimated by government; the language of 'transformation' is inappropriate for a long, slow process which may take more than a decade to complete; the battery of mechanisms selected to 'deliver' such change has proved too mechanical; and the climate of fear which permeates the sector must give way to a climate of mutual trust.

Can this disorganised, troubled but pivotal sector still be turned into a learning system? That would require politicians and policy makers to change some of their fundamental beliefs and practices and to think and talk differently; institutions to reorder their priorities in favour of pedagogy; and professionals to be given the space and resources to improve their existing expertise. The chances are very slim, but it could be done.

Coda

Finally, I want to break a rhetorical convention, even if Demosthenes chokes on one of his pebbles as a result, by emphasising an idea right at the end of this talk, which has run like a *leitmotiv* through it. I want to go back to my first research project on Glasgow gangs and present two photos that I took of the area those boys came from. The worst slums have long since gone, but we have built grim housing estates in their place. In this rich country 2.4 million children still live in poverty, and the gap between the rich and the poor is greater now than when I started work. The government is slowly realising that, despite new buildings and extra resources, many of the city academies are failing because they are situated in areas of ingrained multiple deprivation which education alone cannot solve. We have a collective responsibility for such conditions, and the link between social class and low educational attainment will never be broken until we take that responsibility far more seriously than we have ever done. We need new arrangements to transfer resources from relatively advantaged to disadvantaged areas, from the rich to the poor. This is the central political and moral challenge for this generation and we must rise to meet it because it is a matter of social justice. We need a politics of serious and sustained redistribution.

Acknowledgements

The word 'gratitude' is not enough to express my thanks to Tony Edwards, that peerless commentator, who improved an earlier version of this talk. I am also grateful to Keith Mitchell, Ron Glatter, Phil Hodkinson and Douglas Weir for pointing out weaknesses.

Notes

1.	The researchers wish to acknowledge with gratitude the funding of this project by the ESRC (reference number RES-139-25-0105).
2.	The research team consisted of Sheila Edward, Ian Finlay, Maggie Gregson, Ann Hodgson, Ken Spours, Richard Steer, Louise Wilson and Jo Lakey.
3.	Newman's framework places the four types of governance on two dimensions. The vertical axis represents the degree to which power is centralised or decentralised, while the horizontal axis depicts the orientation towards continuity or change. The resulting four quadrants produce four models of governance – the hierarchical model, the rational-goal model, the open-systems model and the self-governance model. Current government policy for the sector is not concentrated in any one or two of the quadrants but is scattered throughout all four. For instance, the standardisation of teaching materials by the Standards Unit is firmly within the hierarchical model, but its regional networks of subject coaches belong to the self-governance model because the coaches are meant to be agents of self-improvement; the focus on targets, goals and performance indicators is a good example of the rational-goal model; the devolution of responsibility for achieving outcomes to the 'frontline' is characteristic of the open-systems model; while the long-term investment in staff training and the proposed move to self-regulation are part and parcel of the self-governance model.
4.	A list of the more significant initiatives since 1997 would include: *Skills for Life* (DfEE, 2001) to improve the literacy, numeracy and language skills of adults. By the end of 2005, 1.25 million adults had acquired a qualification in literacy, numeracy or language at a cost of £2 billion (see Sherlock, 2005). A series of pilots called the Employer Training Programme, where government funded the training chosen by employers, has become a national measure entitled Train to Gain. The Employer Training pilots helped over 29,000 businesses and enabled 240,000 employees to gain vocational qualifications. The new National Employer Training Programme, to be known as Train to Gain, will cost £288 million in 2006–7 and £457 million in 2007–8 (DfESa, 2006: 38); and is forecast to benefit 50,000 employers and 350,000 employees each year (HMT, 2006: 64). Foundation degrees, which are normally completed within two years full-time, have 25,000 students currently in FE colleges; the Increased Flexibility Programme, which enables up to 80,000 14–16-year-olds to sample vocational courses in FE colleges; Education Maintenance Allowances, which provide 16–19-year-olds from poor families with up to £30 per week while they study. More than 400,000 students were receiving EMAs in the academic year 2005–6 (Hook, 2006) at a cost of £511 million. Entry to Employment, which offers access to Level 1 provision and below to those aged 16–18; a skill academy for each of the major sectors of the economy; Union Learning Representatives (estimated at 12,000 in December 2005) with statutory recognition to encourage workmates back into learning; the University for Industry and learndirect, which help people to find the courses they want via the internet or telephone and provide courses in ICT, management and basic skills; a Standards Unit in the DfES to identify and spread 'best practice' in vocational subjects; 403 Centres of Vocational Excellence (CoVEs) in FE colleges, with expertise in a particular vocational area; a

reformed system of apprenticeships, with Young Apprenticeships for students aged 14–16, Apprenticeship to Level 2, Advanced Apprenticeships to Level 3 and Adult Apprenticeships for those 25 and over. (The number of apprenticeships has tripled to over 250,000 since 1997.)

5. The Leitch Report also included a chart of the major organisations in the sector which contains 45 entries and still has to add the caution that 'some institutions have been omitted' (2005: 114).

6. 'Their ability to raise revenue [was] cut from 60 per cent to 25 per cent, some £30 billion of services transferred to unelected quangos, and its other services micromanaged from the centre' (*Guardian* leader, 16 December 2005).

7. A recent consultation paper from the Office of the Deputy Prime Minister 'describes a selection of the huge range of existing partnerships which exist at local level, which is by no means exhaustive' (ODPM, 2005: 28). Annex B in that paper lists 24 different partnerships in each locality in the six main areas of: children and young people; safer communities; crime and disorder reduction; economic development and enterprise; healthier communities; and the environment. Interestingly, lifelong learning is not one of the main sub-groups. The 360 local strategic partnerships (LSPs) in England are to become 'the partnership of partnerships in an area, providing the strategic co-ordination within the area and linking with other plans and bodies established at the regional, sub-regional and local level' (ibid.: 11). If each of the 360 LSPs oversees a minimum of 24 partnerships, then a conservative estimate for the total number of local partnerships in England is 8,640.

8. I have just started a new project to appraise critically the evidential basis of this model of reform. I wish to acknowledge the financial support of the Director and the Dean of Research within the Institute of Education.

9. Kooiman, for example, has argued that there has been a general shift among governments away from 'one way traffic' to 'two way traffic', where 'aspects, qualities, problems and opportunities of both the governing system and the system to be governed are taken into consideration' (quoted by Newman, 2001: 15).

10. In 1999, the Cabinet Office issued a report on Modernising Government which stipulated that 'Government should regard policy-making as a continuous learning process, not a series of one-off initiatives.… Feedback from those who implement and deliver policies and services is essential'. Quoted by Newman (2001: 63). Ministers know what they should do, but the culture of momentum politics and the need to make their mark quickly both militate against them accepting such advice.

11. The following definition of learning was developed by colleagues in the ESRC's Learning Society Programme: Learning refers only to significant changes in capability, understanding, attitudes or values by individuals, groups, organisations or society. It excludes the acquisition of further information when it does not contribute to such changes. Alternatively, Etienne Wenger defines learning as 'a realignment of experience and competence' (1998: 227).

12. It talks of developing 'a suite of measures to be published regularly' to assess not only the performance of colleges 'but show how the LSC is doing too – locally, regionally and nationally' (2005: 18).

13. 'We have had six Asylum and Immigration Ministers so far, seven Europe Ministers, nine Ministers with responsibility for entry clearance, of whom I was also one, and the

Department of Health has been more or less cleaned out twice in the past 18 months or so. I know that decisions on such matters are for people far above my pay grade, but I gently wonder whether that is the most efficient use of resources and officials' time and whether we get the best out of people by reshuffling the pack with such terrifying rapidity'. Chris Mullin, speech in House of Commons, Foreign Affairs and Defence, 18 May 2005.

14. Dr Kim Howells, George Mudie, Malcolm Wicks, John Healey, Margaret Hodge, Alan Johnston and Bill Rammell.
15. The Scottish Parliament, the National Assembly for Wales, the Mayor and Assembly for London are clear examples of the former, as are the new institutions such as the regional development agencies, local strategic partnerships, the local LSCs and the urban regeneration companies. On the other hand, the establishment of Government Offices of the Regions was more concerned with the efficient, local 'delivery' of central policy than strengthening either regional or local government. Moreover, the academies and the proposed new foundation schools are being set up independently of local accountability, and so will seriously constrain local area planning.
16. The proposed re-organisation of 43 police authorities in England and Wales into 12 regional forces is part of the same pattern, but at the same time the Police and Justice Bill (2006) increases the power of the Home Secretary to intervene in poorly performing divisions.
17. In November 2004, 78 per cent of voters in the North East, on a turnout of 48 per cent, rejected a directly elected Regional Assembly.
18. For example, Sunderland Council has developed a distinctive model where three academies will work in partnership with all other schools and the FE college.
19. Forty per cent of the current employees are over 50 and only 20 per cent are under 35 (Hunter, 2005).
20. The interim report of the Leitch review of skills summarised the position as follows: 'In 2005, most agencies responsible for identifying or delivering skills are less than ten years old and still finding their feet as stand-alone institutions or as part of emerging partnerships at national, regional and local levels' (2005: 151).
21. In 2006–7, the LSC had a budget of £10.5 billion and the research budget of the Learning and Skills Research Centre was £1 million, i.e. 0.009 per cent.

References

Ball, S.J., Maguire, M. and Macrae, S. (2000) *Choice, Pathways and Transitions Post-16*. London: RoutledgeFalmer.
—— (2003) 'The teacher's soul and the terrors of performativity'. *Journal of Education Policy*, 18, 2, 215–28.

—— (2005) 'Radical policies, progressive modernisation and deepening democracy: the Academies programme in action'. *Forum*, 47, 2 & 3, 215–22.

Bartlett, W., Rees, T. and Watts, A.G. (2000) *Adult Guidance Services and the Learning Society*. Bristol: Policy Press.

Bernstein, B. (1996) *Pedagogy, Symbolic Control and Identity: Theory, research, critique*. London: Taylor & Francis.

Blair, T. (2005) 'We must never concede the politics of aspiration for all'. *Guardian*, 18 November.

Blunkett, D. (2000) *Remit letter to Learning and Skills Council*, London: DfES.

– (2006) *The Blunkett Tapes: My life in the bear pit*, London: Bloomsbury.

Brine, J. (2006) 'Lifelong learning and the knowledge economy: those that know and those that do not – the discourse of the European Union'. *British Educational Research Journal,* 32, 5, October, 649–65.

Brown, G. (2005) The Hugo Young Memorial Lecture. London: Chatham House, 13 December.

—— (2006) 'We have renewed Britain; now we must champion it'. *Guardian*, 27 February, 32.

Clarke, C. (2004) 'Foreword'. In DfES *Five Year Strategy for Children and Learners: Putting people at the heart of public services*. London: The Stationery Office, Cm 6272, 3–5.

Clarke, J. and Newman, J. (1997) *The Managerial State*. London: Sage.

Coffield, F. (1982) 'Cycles of deprivation'. Durham: University of Durham.

—— (1992) 'Training and Enterprise Councils: the last throw of voluntarism?' *Policy Studies*, 13, 4, 11–32.

—— (1999) 'Breaking the consensus: lifelong learning as social control'. Newcastle: University of Newcastle.

—— (2004) 'Alternative routes out of the low skills equilibrium: a rejoinder to Lloyd and Payne'. *Journal of Education Policy*, 19, 6, November, 733–40.

Coffield, F. and Edward, S. (forthcoming) '"Good", "Best" and now "Excellent" Practice. What next? Perfect Practice?'

Coffield, F., Steer, R., Hodgson, A., Spours, K., Edward, S. and Finlay, I. (2005) 'A new learning and skills landscape? The central role of the Learning and Skills Council'. *Journal of Education Policy*, 20, 5, 631–56.

Department for Communities and Local Government (2006) *Strong and Prosperous Communities: The Local Government White Paper*. London: The Stationery Office, Cm 6939–I and II.

DfEE (1998) *The Learning Age: A renaissance for a new Britain*. London: The Stationery Office, Cm 3790.

—— (2001) Skills for Life: *The National Strategy for Improving Adult Literacy and Numeracy Skills*. Nottingham: DfEE.

DfES (2002) *Success for All: Reforming Further Education and Training: Our Vision for the Future*. London: DfES, November.

—— (2003) *21st Century Skills: Realising Our Potential*. London: Stationery Office, Cm 5810.

—— (2004) *Five Year Strategy for Children and Learners: Putting people at the heart of public services*. London: The Stationery Office, Cm 6272.

—— (2005a) *14–19 Education and Skills*. London: The Stationery Office, Cm 6476.

—— (2005b) *Skills: Getting on in business, getting on at work*. London: The Stationery Office, Cm 6483-11.

—— (2005c) *Higher Standards, Better Schools for All: more choice for parents and pupils*. London: The Stationery Office, Cm 6677.

—— (2006a) *Further Education: Raising Skills, Improving Life Chances*. London: The Stationery Office, Cm 6768.

—— (2006b) *The Five Year Strategy for Children and Learners: Maintaining the Excellent Progress*. Sherwood Park, Annesley, Notts: DfES Publications.

Eagle, A. (2006) 'Make up your mind on education'. *Guardian*, 15 March.

Edwards, T. (1997) 'Educating leaders and training followers'. In A.D. Edwards, T. Edwards, R. Haywood, F. Hardman, N. Meagher, C. Fitzgibbons (eds) *Separate but Equal? A Levels and GNVQs*. London: Routledge, 8–28.

—— (2001) 'Educational performance, markets and the state: present and future prospects'. In R. Phillips and J. Furlong (eds) *Education, Reform and the State: Twenty-five years of politics, policy and practice*. London: RoutledgeFalmer, 239–53.

EEF (2006) *Learning to Change: why the UK skills system must do better*. London: EEF.

Fielding, M. (2006) 'Leadership, personalization and high performance schooling: naming the new totalitarianism'. *School Leadership and Management*, 26, 4, September, 347–69.

Finlay, I., Gregson, M., Spours, K. and Coffield, F. (2005) 'The heart of what we do': policies in teaching, learning and assessment in the new Learning and Skills Sector'. Paper presented at BERA Conference, Glamorgan University, September.

Fletcher, M. and Owen, G. (2005) *The Funding Gap: Funding in schools and colleges for full-time students aged 16–18*. London: LSDA.

Foster, A. (2005) *Realising the Potential: a review of the future role of further education colleges*. London: DfES.

Gewirtz, S., Ball, S.J. and Bowe, R. (1995) *Markets, Choice and Equity in Education*. Buckingham: Open University Press.

Glatter, R. (2003) 'Governance and Educational Innovation'. In B. Davies, and J. West-Burnham (eds) *Handbook of Educational Leadership and Management*. London: Pearson.

Grubb, W.N. (1999) *Honored but Invisible: An inside look at teaching in community colleges*. New York: Routledge.

Guile, D. and Young, M. (2003) 'Transfer and Transition in Vocational Education: Some theoretical considerations'. In T. Tuomi-Gröhn and Y. Engeström (eds) *Between School and Work: New perspectives on transfer and boundary-crossing*. Oxford: Elsevier, 63–81.

HM Treasury (2001) *Pre Budget Report: Building a stronger, fairer Britain in an uncertain world*. London: The Stationery Office, Cm 5318.

—— (2003) *Pre-budget Report*. London: Stationery Office.

—— (2006) *Budget 2006, A Strong and Strengthening Economy: Investing in Britain's Future*, HC968. London: The Stationery Office.

Hodgson, A., Spours, K., Coffield, F., Steer, R., Finlay, I., Edward, S. and Gregson, M. (2005) *A New Learning and Skills Landscape? The LSC within the Learning and Skills Sector*. London: Institute of Education.

Hodgson, A. *et al*. (forthcoming) 'Learners in the English Learning and Skills sector: the implications of half-right policy assumptions'. *Oxford Review of Education*.

Hodkinson, P., Biesta, G. and James, D. (2006) 'Principles of procedure for improving learning'. Online: www.ex.ac.uk/sell/tlc/publications.htm.

Hodkinson, P., Biesta, G. and James, D. (forthcoming) 'Learning cultures and a cultural theory of learning'. *Educational Review*.

Hook, S. (2006) 'More than 380,000 teens are paid to learn'. *Times Educational Supplement, FE Focus*, 6 January, 3.

House of Commons Education and Skills Committee (2006) *The Schools White Paper: Higher standards, better schools for all*. First Report of Session 2005–06, Volume 1, HC 633-1, London: The Stationery Office.

Hunter, D. (2005) 'Boosting skills begins with the teachers'. *Times Educational Supplement, FE Focus*, 16 December.

Hyman, P. (2005) *1 Out of 10: From Downing Street Vision to Classroom Reality*. London: Vintage.

Johnson, A. (2006) *LSC Grant Letter: 2007:08*. London: DfES.

Karabel, J. and Halsey, A.H. (1977) (eds) *Power and Ideology in Education*. New York: Oxford University Press.

Keep, E. (2006) 'State control of the English education and training system – playing with the biggest trainset in the world'. *Journal of Vocational Education and Training*, 58, 1, 47–64.

—— (forthcoming) 'The English vocational and education system: organising the structures, structuring the organisations. A challenge for the central state'.

Kelly, R. (2005a) 'Ministerial foreword'. In DfES (2005) *National Skills Academies: Prospectus 2005/6; An innovative approach to meeting employers' needs for training*. London: DfES.

—— (2005b) Grant letter: 2006–07. London: DfES, 30 October.

Kooiman, J. (2003) *Governing as Governance*. London: Sage.

Leitch, S. (2005) *Skills in the UK: The long-term challenge*, Interim Report. London: HM Treasury.

—— (2006) *Prosperity for all in the global economy – world class skills*, Final Report. London: Stationery Office.

Lowndes, V., Pratchett, L. and Stoker, G. (2006) *Locality Matters: Making participation count in local politics*. London: IPPR.

LSC (2005a) *A Clear Direction, Annual Report and Accounts*, 2004–05. Coventry: LSC.

—— (2005b) *Learning and Skills – the agenda for change*. Coventry: LSC, August.

—— (2006a) *New Measures of Success*, Letter to providers. Coventry: LSC, 6 January.

—— (2006b) *Framework for Excellence: A comprehensive assessment performance framework for the further education system*. Coventry: LSC.

Mortimore, P. (2006) *Which Way Forward? An education system for the 21st century*. London: NUT.

Mortimore, P. and Whitty, G. (2000) *Can School Improvement Overcome the Effects of Disadvantage?* London: Institute of Education.

Mulgan, G. (2006) 'Central reservations'. *Society Guardian*, 1 March, 10.

Newman, J. (2000) 'Beyond the new public management? Modernising public services'. In J. Clarke, S. Gewirtz and E. McLaughlin (eds) *New managerialism, New Welfare?* London: Sage/Open University.

—— (2001) *Modernising Governance: New Labour, policy and society*. London: Sage.

—— (2005) (ed.) *Remaking Governance: Peoples, politics and the public sphere*. Bristol: Policy Press.

NIACE (2005) *Eight in Ten: Adult learners in further education*. Leicester: NIACE.

OECD (2006) *Education at a Glance: OECD Indicators 2006*. Paris: OECD.

Office of the Deputy Prime Minister (2005) *Local Strategic Partnerships: Shaping their future*. London: ODPM.

O'Neil, O. (2002) Reith Lectures. London: BBC.

PMSU (Prime Minister's Strategy Unit) (2006) *The UK Government's Approach to Public Service Reform: A discussion paper.* London: Strategy Unit.

Power, M. (1997) *The audit society: rituals of verification.* Oxford: Oxford University Press.

QIA (2006) *Pursuing Excellence: An outline improvement strategy for consultation.* Coventry: QIA.

Raffe, D. (2002) 'The issues, some reflections and possible next steps'. In Nuffield Foundation (ed.) *14–19 Education.* London: Nuffield Foundation.

Raffe, D. *et al.* (forthcoming) 'The Impact of a Unified Curriculum and Qualifications System: The Higher Skill Reform of Post–16 Education in Scotland'. *British Educational Research Journal.*

Sarason, S. (1990) *The Predictable Failure of Educational Reform: Can we change course before it's too late?* San Francisco: Jossey-Bass.

Scott, J.C. (1998) *Seeing Like a State: How certain schemes to improve the human condition have failed.* New Haven: Yale University Press.

Sennett, R. (1998) *The Corrosion of Character: The personal consequences of work in the new capitalism.* New York: W. W. Norton.

Sherlock, D. (2005) *Annual Report of the Chief Inspector.* Coventry: ALI.

Skelcher, C. (1998) *The Appointed State.* Buckingham: Open University Press.

Stanton, G. and Fletcher, M. (2006) '14–19 institutional arrangements in England – research perspective on collaboration, competition and patterns of post-16 provision'. Nuffield Review of 14–19 Education and Training, Working Paper 38. Online: *www.nuffield14–19review.org.uk.*

Thompson, A. (2006) 'The Quality Improvement Agency for Lifelong Learning'. Standards Unit Conference, Newcastle Racecourse, 27 January.

Wenger, E. (1998) *Communities of Practice: Learning, meaning and identity.* Cambridge: Cambridge University Press.

Whitty, G. (1997) 'Marketization, the state and the re-formation of the teaching profession'. In A.H. Halsey, H. Lauder, P. Brown, and A.S. Wells (eds) *Education: Culture, Economy, Society.* Oxford: Oxford University Press.

Williams, R. (1983) *Towards 2000.* London: Chatto and Windus.

Wolf, A. (2002) *Does Education Matter? Myths about education and economic growth.* London: Penguin.